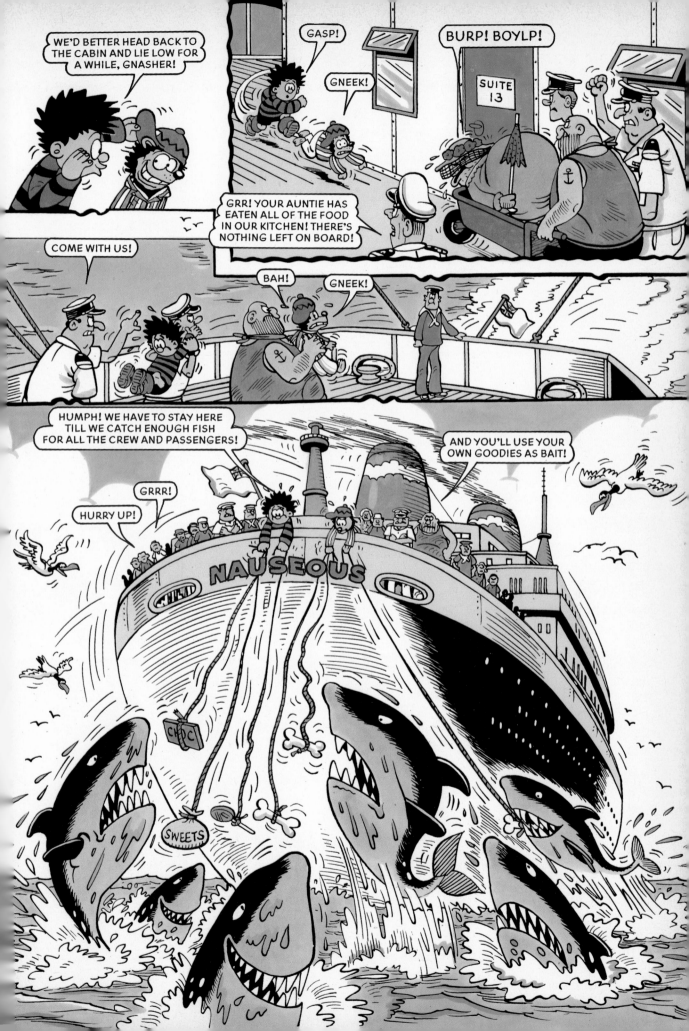

IVY THE TERRIBLE

OH, NO! I'VE GOT TO CLEAN THE HOUSE. YOU KNOW WHAT THAT MEANS!

I'LL HELP!

ER, FOUND THAT GOBSTOPPER I LOST IN 1993.

HELP? HELP? YOU MADE ALL THIS MESS, IVY!

TRUE!

THE BEANO

I'LL DO SOME DUSTING FOR YOU, THEN.

IF YOU MUST. HERE'S A DUSTER!

SCOOT!

Soon—

IT'S OKAY! I'VE MADE MY OWN.

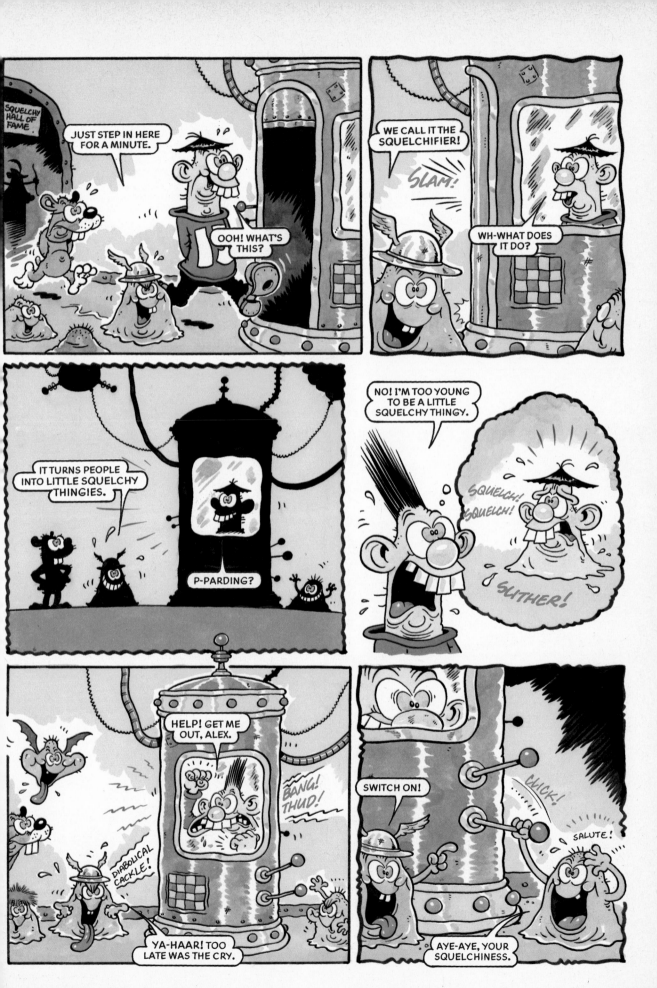

The NUMSKULLS

EYE DEPT.

WHAT A LOVELY CHRISTMAS TREE.

WISH WE HAD ONE!

WE WILL! I HAVE A CUNNING PLAN TO GET A TREE. FIRST, WE'LL SEND EDD TO THE SHOPS.

GOOD. THIS PLACE NEEDS BRIGHTENING UP!

So —

GONNA TAKE ME TO THE SHOPS FOR SWEETS, MUM?

SURE, EDD.

AHA! THE CAR AIR FRESHENER IS WHAT WE NEED.

LUCKY EDD HAD SPAGHETTI FOR LUNCH.

TUM DEPT.

TO BRAIN DEPT.

LOOP!

GOTTIT!

DON'T WORRY THAT IT'S NOT DECORATED, NUMSKULLS.

EAR DEPT.

'DRAG!

Sweets

I'M GOING TO BUY MY FAVES!

SLOBBER!

YUMMEE

JELLY TOTS

YUM-YUM-YUM-YUM-YUM-AND DELISH!

GUZZLE! GLURK!

THERE! LOVELY TREE. ISN'T IT?

MOUTH DEPT.

WHIFF OF FRESH!

YOU BET.

AND EDD WON'T HAVE BAD BREATH OVER CHRISTMAS!

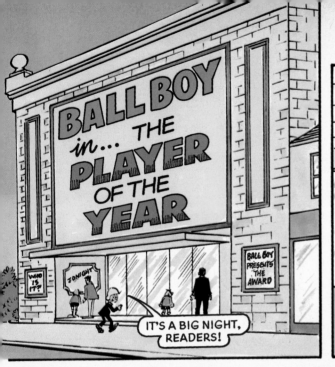

BALL BOY in... THE PLAYER OF THE YEAR

IT'S A BIG NIGHT, READERS!

I'M GOING TO PRESENT THE 'PLAYER OF THE YEAR' AWARD. BET I HAVE TO PRESENT IT TO MYSELF! HA-HA!

Soon—

MY LORDS, LADIES AND GENTLEMEN . . .

WHO — US? LORDS? HA-HA!

GENTLEMEN? NO WAY! HO-HO!

IT'S BEEN A BIT OF A DISAPPOINTING SEASON.

TRUE — YOU'RE RUBBISH!

WORSE THAN ARBROATH!

YOU COULDN'T WIN A RAFFLE!

IN THE LEAGUE, OUR FAILURE IN FRONT OF GOAL COST US DEAR.

SMASH!

MISS!

CRASH!

CRASH!

OOPS!

OH, DEAR!

YIKES!

The BASH STREET KIDS

WAA! THERE'S A BIG DOG AFTER ME! HELP!

ZOOM

IT WON'T GO AWAY!

ER . . . SMIFFY!

EH? WHAT'S GOING ON HERE? I CAN'T SEE A THING!

S-UCK!

GREAT WORK, FIDO!

HUMPH! I CAN'T FIND MY GLASSES OR THE TEST PAPERS! WHAT A DAY!

BLAST!

OKAY — TIME FOR P.E.! TO THE GYM HALL, KIDS!

THUD!

LIFT!

WELL DONE, KIDS! EVEN YOU MANAGED IT, FATTY!

But.

CRACK

CRACK

PING

?

NO, HEADMASTER!

SO! YOU LOT DO HAVE HIM!

OH, THAT ELEPHANT! CHORTLE!

SUCK!

HUH! IF YOU WEREN'T SO LAZY, TEACHER — YOU WOULD HAVE SPOTTED IT!

GYM HALL

DAZED!

GENERAL JUMBO

Jumbo Johnson was the proud owner of an army of special radio-controlled models. Jumbo had taken a small detachment of his force into Northumbria when he went to visit his cousin Amy —

THE ROMAN WALL'S A GREAT PLACE TO DRILL YOUR ARMY, JUMBO.

YEAH — I WISH I HAD BROUGHT MORE, BUT I COULD ONLY BRING A SMALL PART FROM HOME.

COME AND MEET A FEW FRIENDS OF MINE.

THEY LOOK HARD AT WORK.

HOW'S THE RE-BUILDING OF THE WALL GOING?

WE COULD DO WITH A HAND.

MAYBE I COULD HELP?

And —

THAT'S FOR SCRATCHING MY PAINTWORK.

CACKLE! NO CONTEST!

YOU BUNCH OF WIMPS ARE A PUSHOVER!

WE'LL BE BACK!

MY MODELS ARE WRECKED!

SO IS ALL THE WORK WE'VE DONE TO THE WALL.

THEY'LL BE BACK, EH? WELL, I'LL BE WAITING — THIS MEANS WAR!

Back to Amy's cottage —

EVEN IF WE FIX YOUR MODELS, THEY'RE NO MATCH FOR JEREMY'S GO-KARTS!

THIS CALLS FOR DIFFERENT TACTICS!

Jumbo phones Professor Carter, the inventor of the models —

. . . CAN YOU SEND WHAT'S NEEDED, PROFESSOR?

REINFORCEMENTS ON THEIR WAY, JUMBO.

JUMBO

Next day — at the railway station —

WHAT'S BEEN SENT, JUMBO? BIGGER TANKS? MISSILES? GUNSHIPS?

ROCKET LAUNCHERS? STEALTH BOMBERS?

ROMAN SOLDIERS!

SOMETHING **MUCH** MORE EFFECTIVE!

WHEN IN NORTHUMBRIA . . .! AND ALL THAT!

Back to work on the wall —

WE'LL REPAIR THE DAMAGE DONE YESTERDAY.

And, of course, soon enough —

THOSE WIMPS ARE BACK!

LET'S **REALLY** SCARE 'EM, THIS TIME, CHAPS!

But, as Jeremy and his fellows move towards the wall —

WHERE DID THEY POP UP FROM?

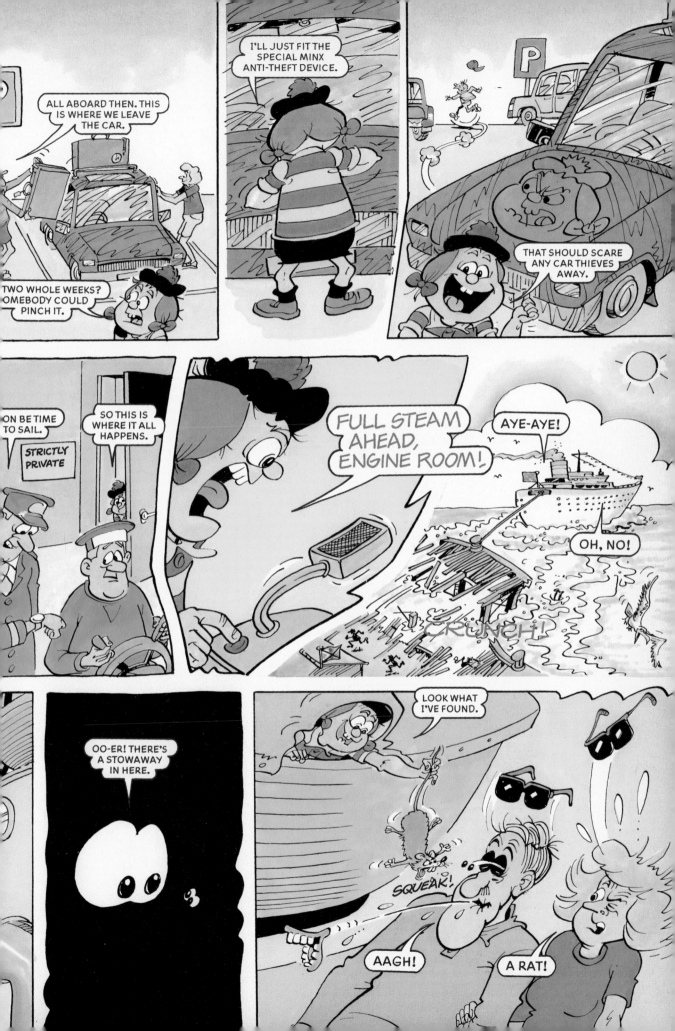

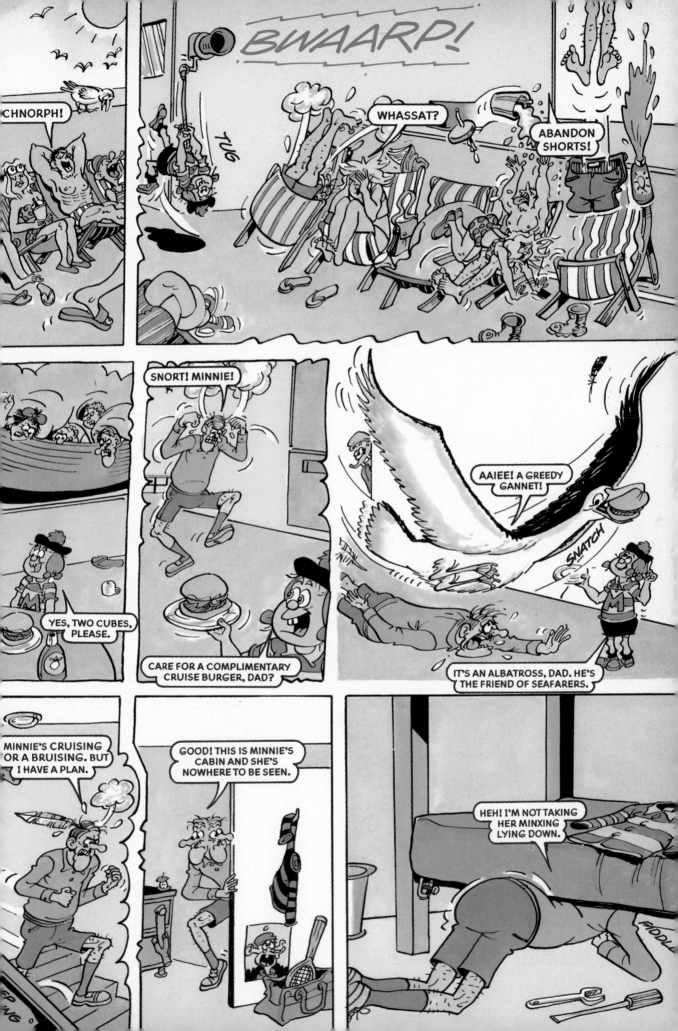

Gnasher and Gnipper

TIP!

THERE'S MORE THAN ONE USE FOR A BONE!

Golf Clubs

GFORE!

PLASTIC GOLF BALLS

Snooker Clues.

BRUSSEL SPROUTS!

I INVENTED THIS GAME TO GET RID OF THOSE SPROUTS!

Drumsticks.

A bike.

GWOW! A REAL BONE SHAKER!

GNIP!

SHAKE!

RATTLE!

Xylophone.

GNEE-HEE!

GWAYEY!

PLINK!

✦✦✦ STARG

CAPRICORN *(SPOTTY)*

THE GOAT IS MY STAR-SIGN.
GOATS' FACES ARE GROTTY.
SO I MADE ONE HANDSOME
BY PAINTING HIM SPOTTY.

AQUARIUS *(PLUG)*

I'M THE WATER CARRIER –
THE BEST LOOKING MALE.
BUT FOLK SAY I'M CUTER
WEARING MY PAIL.

TAURUS *(FATTY)*

I'M A BIG GUY CALLED FATTY,
AS LARGE AS A BULL.
I DOUBLE MY WEIGHT,
WHEN MY TUMMY IS FULL.

GEMINI *(WINSTON)*

I'M WINSTON–A COOL CAT,
MY STAR SIGN'S THE TWINS.
SO I MAKE A STAND-IN
SCOFF-OLIVE'S DIN-DINS.

VIRGO *(SMIFFY)*

MY STAR SIGN IS VIRGO,
I DON'T THINK IT'S FAIR.
THAT THEY SHOULD NAME SIGNS
AFTER SOME SNOOKER PLAYER.

SCORPIO *(DANNY)*

I'M DANNY, THE SCORPION,
WITH A STING IN THE TAIL.
A PIRATE BY INSTINCT,
WHEN HEADMASTER SETS SAIL.

AZERS

PISCES ('ERBERT)

I'M 'ERBERT THE FISH,
I LOVE ANGLING FOR COD.
BUT I CAN'T GET A BITE
ON MY TRUSTY OLD ROD.

ARIES (WILFRID)

I'M WILFRID THE RAM,
WOOLLY OVER MY CHIN.
EVEN TOP X-FILES AGENTS
DON'T KNOW WHAT'S WITHIN.

CANCER (CUTHBERT)

I'M CUTHBERT, THE CRAB.
CRINGEWORTHY, THAT'S ME.
I'M AN EXPERT AT CRAWLING,
I'M THE SWAT OF 2B.

LEO (SIDNEY)

I'M SO LION HEARTED,
AND SIDNEY'S MY NAME.
MY HAIR IS MUCH TOUGHER
THAN LEO'S OLD MANE.

SAGITTARIUS (TOOTS)

I'M MAID TOOTS, THE ARCHER,
WITH BOW AND WITH ARROWS.
MY FAVOURITE TARGETS
ARE TEACHER'S PRIZE MARROWS.

LIBRA (OLIVE)

I'M OLIVE THE SCHOOL COOK,
I BALANCE MY SCALES.
TO MAKE SURE MY STEW HAS
ENOUGH SLIME AND SNAILS.

ROAR!

EEK! WHATEVER IT IS, I DON'T LIKE IT.

Some added buffalo hair later —

BIGFOOT NOW HAS HIS COAT IN PERFECT CONDITION.

MM! BIGFOOT SMELL BIG FOOD.

AROMA ~

WHERE'S LES GOT TO? HE LOVES SAUSAGES AND BEANS.

NEVER MIND HIM. WHERE ARE MY BOOTS?

UGG! UGG!

SCREAM! WHAT IS THAT, DAD?

IT'S B-BIGFOOT! LES HAS A BOOK ABOUT HIM.

WELL, HE CERTAINY LIKES MY COOKING. TUCK IN — IT'LL PUT HAIR ON YOUR CHEST.

AND HE LIKES MY BOOTS, TOO.

Shortly —

HUH? LOGGERS COME TO DESTROY BIGFOOT'S FOREST HOME.

DRR!

DRRR!

DRR!

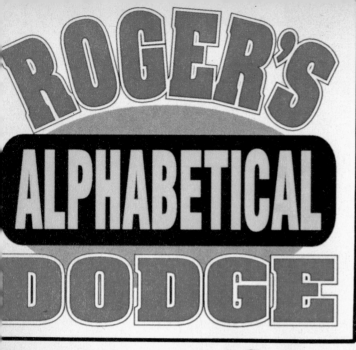

ROGER'S ALPHABETICAL DODGE

AAARGH!

DETECTOR

EAGLE-EYED-B

HAVE A SMALL REWARD

IDEA

Boo-hoo!

Cocky or what?

Falling metal

Good thinking

JOKE Shop

Joke shop

TOMATO KETCHUP

Ketchup bottle

LAUNDERETTE

LAUNDERETTE

ROAD WORKS

MAJOR ROADWORKS

OFF BLOWS HIS TOP

PLURP GOES THE KETCHUP

BUS STOP

STRAIGHT OVER TO Q

TAXI

NEUMATIC DRILL (THE 'P' IS SILENT)

Q GETS IT

(THE 'W' IS SILENT)

RIGGLES OUT OF BOTTLE

USHERS THEM INTO LAUNDERETTE

VERY GOOD FOR BUSINESS

WHOPPING BIG REWARD

XTRA BIG FEED

YOU WON'T BELIEVE THIS

BAM! BAM! BAM!

ZERO KETCHUP

EVEN STEVEN

HE'S OUT FOR REVENGE

Our story begins —

YEAH! SYDNEY! I'VE ALWAYS FANCIED SYDNEY!

IT'S S!DNEY, ACTUALLY, BUT I'LL FORGIVE YOU, DARLIN', FOR YOUR FINE TASTE IN FELLAS!

SCHOOL

BASH STREET SCHOOL

NO, NO! SYDNEY IS WHERE THE OLYMPICS ARE BEING HELD. I LOVE ALL THAT ATHLETICS AND STUFF!

PYOINNG!

DUCK!

THUD!

YEOWP!

JANITORS PRIZE BUSH

SNIP!

GARDEN CANES

YES — IT'S IN AUSTRALIA, ON THE OTHER SIDE OF THE WORLD.

D'YOU FANCY GOING?

YEAH! LET'S GO!

HOWL!

RUB

I'LL GET RID OF THESE DREADFUL KIDS. YES! GO — PLEASE GO!

The quickest suitcase-packing ever, and —

I'M OFF ON A DREAM HOLIDAY — WITH NO KIDS!

ZOOM!

WE'LL INVITE ALL OUR OTHER PALS AS WELL!

THAT DOES IT!

BELCH!

I'M GOING BACK TO WHEN MANNERS WERE IMPORTANT.

THIS LOOKS THE PLACE FOR ME.

GOODE MANOR

PRAY ENTER, YOUNG SIRE.

WHY THANK YOU.

I'LL TETHER YOUR, ER, HORSE, SIRE.

WELCOME, YOUNG FELLOW. HAVE YOU TRAVELLED FAR?

OH, JUST A FEW CENTURIES.

HO-HO! MOST AMUSING.

Now Tim has to watch his own manners —

HMM! WHICH SPOON DO I USE?

RAISE YOUR GOBLETS, EVERYONE.

A TOAST TO OUR YOUNG GUEST.

SO THIS IS WHAT YOU USE FOR SOUP.

SCOOP

THE BASH STREET KIDS

At school.

GASP! IT'S NOT LIKE THE KIDS TO TAKE SHOWERS!

SCHOOL TOWELS

WE'RE NOT SHOWERING, WE'RE GETTING IN THE MOOD FOR OUR SCHOOL FIELD TRIP TO — EGYPT!

Later, at an Egyptian airport...

BEHAVE NOW, YOU LOT!

MUMMY AIRWAYS

TRIP!

THIS TRIP WAS PAID FOR BY THE KIND PEOPLE OF BEANOTOWN. VERY NICE OF THEM! WHEW!

Meanwhile, back in Beanotown.

'NICE'? NO CHANCE! HO-HO!

IT'S A GREAT WAY FOR US TO HAVE A BREAK FROM THOSE NASTY KIDS!

SLIDE!

POP

Back in Egypt_

HOLD ON!

HOI!

SNATCH!

YOU HAVE TO WEAR A FEZ, SIR!

FLOP!

I CAN'T SEE FOR THE SUN!

SNATCH!

I'LL SOON FIX THAT!

EEK!

SPIT

CRASH

SWERVE

ZOOM!

BY THE BEARD OF MY GRANDMOTHER — I CAN'T SEE AT ALL NOW! WAA!

Much later.

HOTEL

SPLAT!

TUG!

TIME TO VISIT THE SIGHTS!

ONE HUMP OR TWO?

EH? TIME FOR TEA?

SQUASH!

HA-HA! ONE 'HUMP' OR TWO, TEACHER? NOT ASKING ABOUT SUGAR LUMPS!

OH, ER . . .

FRED'S FEZ'S

ENGLEESH SPOOKEN HEER

TAXI, SIR?

SPLAT!

SQUASH!

HO-HO! EVEN CARS WEAR A FEZ HERE!

TO OUR HOTEL, PLEASE!

VROOM!

WOW!

YAHOO! OUR HOTEL!

CLINK!

SIGH! THIS HAS COST ME A FORTUNE!

TOSS

HUMPH!

SLIDE!

RECEPT

ER... EXCUSE THE KIDS... JUST HIGH SPIRITS!

HUP! EFFENDI!

TOSS

CHEW

CHEW

BLARE OF MUSIC

AAAGH!

YAHOO!

WAVE!

ZOOM

TRAMPLE!

EH? THREE HUMPS, FATTY?

FLY TRAP

YAHOO!

SPLOT

SPLASH

ZOOM!

WAHEY! FASTER THAN ANY SPEED BOAT!

Later —

I'M NOW IN THE 'MODEL AIRCRAFT' CLUB! I'M GOING TO MAKE A GLIDER TO FLY!

HMM! I CAN FEEL A BIT OF LIFT!

WHEE

SNARL!

AHEM! I THINK I'D BETTER FLY TOO!

HUH! IT'S NO USE! WHIZZSPEED MEANS I CAN NEVER JOIN ANY GROUP!

The performance is almost over.

SWING

LIFT

TOUCH

PARP!

SCREECH

...e not wanting to ...een at the ballet !

HMM! WE HAVEN'T SEEN BILLY ON STAGE YET!

Then —

GET READY TO GO ON FOR THE BIG FINISH, BILLY!

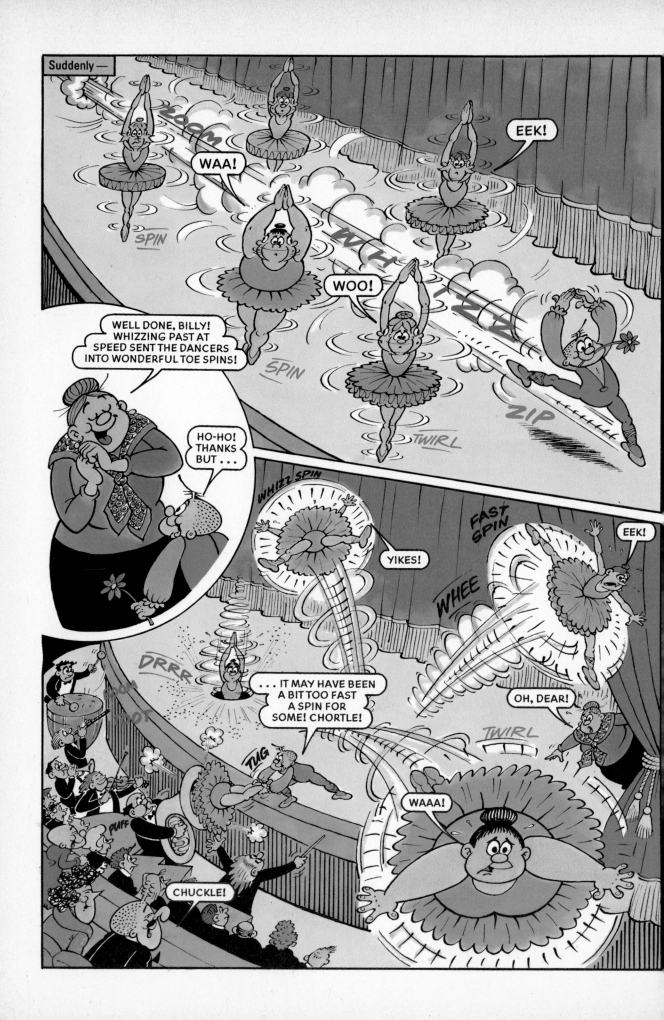

AT EASTER I BOUGHT A GIANT EGG . . .

PONG!

. . . DAISY GAVE ME EGGS TOO — ROTTEN ONES!

ON HER BIRTHDAY I GAVE DAISY A BEAUTIFULLY WRAPPED GIFT . . .

. . . SHE GAVE ME THE WRAPPING BACK!

BOOM!

BANG!

ERNEST LOVES DAISY

FIZZ!

FOR BONFIRE NIGHT I HAD A SPECIAL FIREWORK MADE . . .

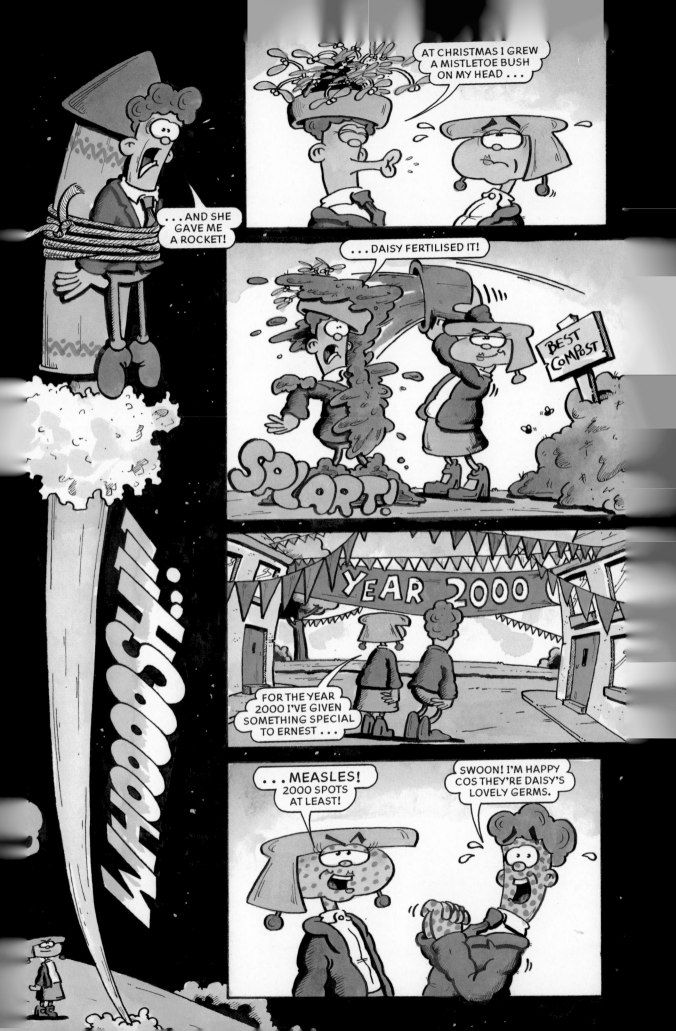

1
OO! OW! SPLUTTER!
CALAMITY JAMES
ERNEST AND DAISY
2
ISN'T THIS GREAT, DAISY?
GRRRR!
THE NUMSKULLS
3
PUSH OFF!
BALL BOY
GOAL!
4
5
UMBRELLAS FOR SALE £50
ROGER THE DODGER
OLIVE THE BASH STREET COOK
GROO!
TRY ONE OF MY HOT DOGS — YOU WON'T GET BETTER!
OLIVE'S HOT DOGS
6
BILLY WHIZZ
7
BURGER BAR
GIFTS
GOLDEN MILE
PRIZES
LES PRETEND
AFTER MY JOB, EH?
8

BALL BOY in... NOTHING EXCITING EVER HAPPENS TO ME!

TA-RAH!

BOOM!

YIKES!

MWAH!

SIGH! NOTHING EXCITING EVER HAPPENS TO ME!

You spoke too soon, Ball Boy!

BALL BOY?

UH? YES!

TODAY, BALL BOY, THIS IS YOUR LIFE!

MICHAEL ASPEL

THIS IS YOUR LIFE

WOW! HOW EXCITING!

Soon, in a T.V. studio —

I REMEMBER BALL BOY STARTED TO KICK EARLY.

WHAT DO YOU MEAN, MUM?

Before Ball Boy was born —

I'LL JUST LISTEN TO THE LITTLE FELLOW!

I THINK HE'S GOING TO BE A FOOTBALL PLAYER! HA-HA!

KICK!

BOP!

HOWL!

Dad next.

I GAVE B.B. A GAME OF BLOW FOOTBALL.

OH-OH! HE'S BLOWING TOO HARD!

PUFF!

I KNEW IT! HE'S HAD AN ACCIDENT.

HONK!

AH! HIS FIRST EARLY BATH!

GROO!

HMM!

I REMEMBER IT WELL.

Ball Boy's Playgroup Teacher now —

B.B. WAS A GOOD SHEPHERD IN OUR NATIVITY PLAY.

TELL US MORE!

'AT IT, WISE MEN. MAKE A WALL!

GOAL! 'SEASY!

SWERVE!

I WAS B.B.'S FIRST COACH.

OH, DEAR!

COACH

ONE MORE ON TOP! WE CAN ALL GET ON THE COACH!

OO! WRONG KIND OF COACH, BALL BOY.

AND I WAS THE FIRST REF BALL BOY CALLED A BLIND OLD BAT.

CHEEKY YOUNG STRIKER!

MAYBE — BUT I'M HERE. THAT'S A PLANT YOU'RE TALKING TO.

Then —

AND WE'RE BALL BOY'S FIRST TEAM.

WAHEY!

AND I REMEMBER THE FIRST CUP WE WON.

CHIP!

TO YOU, B.B. DRIBBLE ON AND SCORE!

Many tantrums later —

WELL, ALL RIGHT! YOU CAN GO OUT IF YOU PUT PLENTY OF THIS ON.

BRONZO SUN CREAM

HMPH!

POWERFUL FRAGRANT PONG!

YUK! I'M NOT PUTTING THIS STUFF ON. I'LL SMELL LIKE A SOFTIE.

SUN OZNO

OR! YUMMY CREAM.

PARK

ERK! YOU LOT CAN BUZZ OFF AS WELL.

BUZZ!

ZOOM!

BUZZ!

TIME TO GET RID OF THE CREAM AND THESE BEES.

SPALOOSH!

Shortly —

JOKE SHOP

OPEN

I'VE GOT A BLISTERING DODGE IDEA.

CHUCKLE! I CAN DO SOME SHADY DODGING IN THIS SOMBRERO, READERS.

Back in the park —

HEY! LEAVE MY BOAT ALONE! BIG BULLIES!

PLOP!

SPLOOSH!

THAT'S NOT VERY NICE.

A SOMBRERO CAN ALSO BE A TEN-GALLON HAT.

WOW! MARTY MOLE AND HIS FAMILY.

SORRY, ROGER, BUT IT'S AWFULLY HOT UNDERGROUND TODAY.

MM! NICE COOL SHOWER.

LITTER

BOOT!

IT'S TIME THOSE TWO WERE TAUGHT A LESSON.

Quality Ice Cream

ICES and LOLLIES

THIS IS MY QUEUE FOR ANOTHER SOMBRERO DODGE.

WHOOSH!

YIKES! A UFO!

GOOD DODGE, EH? AND I DIDN'T TAKE LONG TO PLANET.

The Ballad of CALAMITY JAMES

The unluckiest lad you've ever ....

Took a stroll towards Number **13**

They took one look as James came .... ~~FAR~~

And quivered and quaked in total ....

For they had heard of the lad's bad .....

And beneath a table, they did ....

"Pretend we've all gone on a ....

And maybe we'll give him the ....

As James stepped up and rang the ....

Upon his ugly nut, it ......

T'was firmly jammed o'er his big ....

He couldn't see to front, or ....

He wobbled and staggered towards the ....

One step further — and missed the ....

Flailing around, James took a ....

Arms and legs in a frightful .....

SECOND-HAND BARGAINS

And now, dear readers, quite a ....

James head-butted a "sleeping" ....

"That's my pet, Sabre!" hear Frankie ....

As past his head, the thing did ....

"That's the Keystone" said Dad, 'neath the ......

As the building now looked very un- ....

With a CRASH, it collapsed, that once proud ....

All left standing, was the door, and a ....

"We have no home! It's been knocked ......

Wailed Fiendish, one unhappy ....

"I have no place to lay my ....

So look who's ended in CJ's ....

Joe King's CREATURE FEATURE

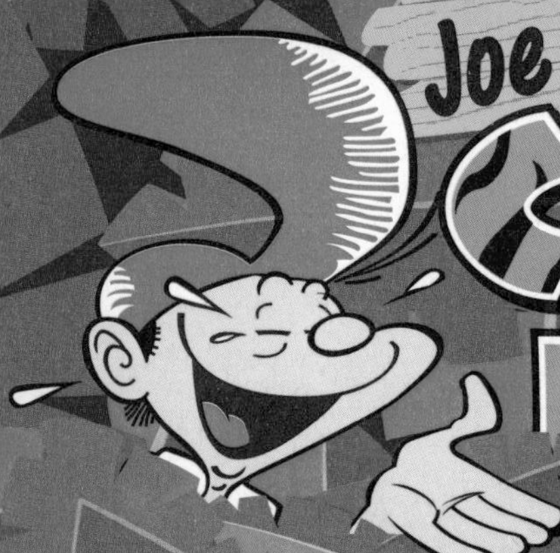

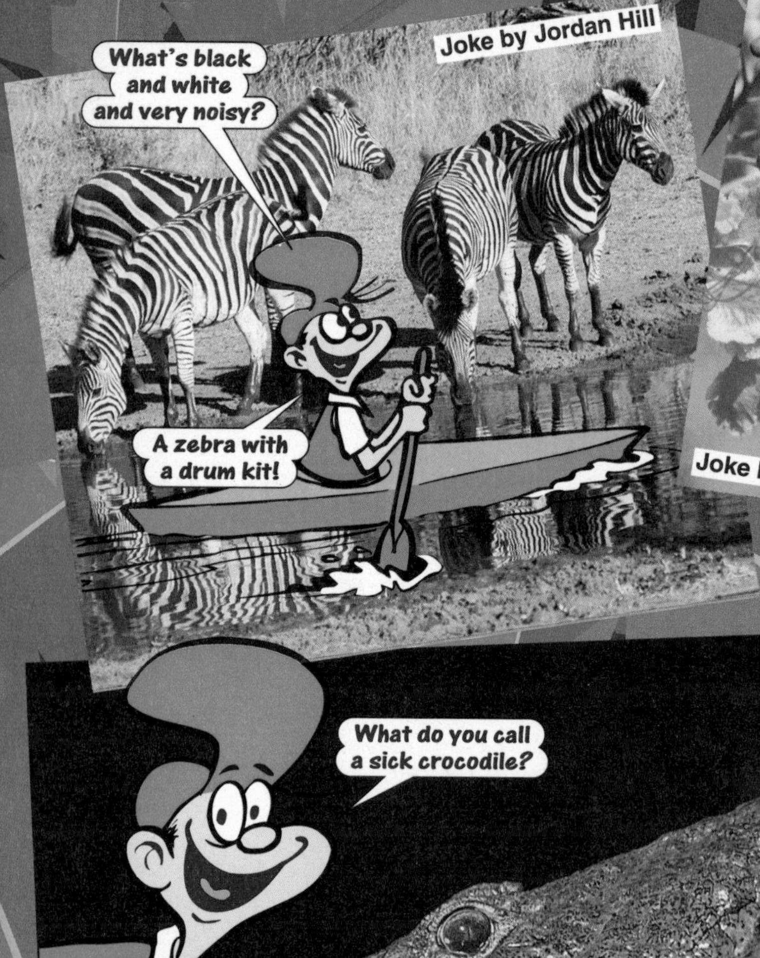

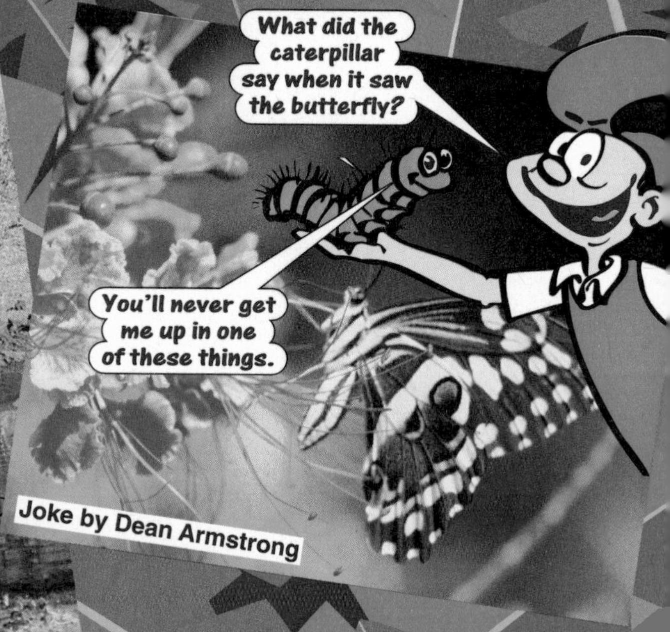

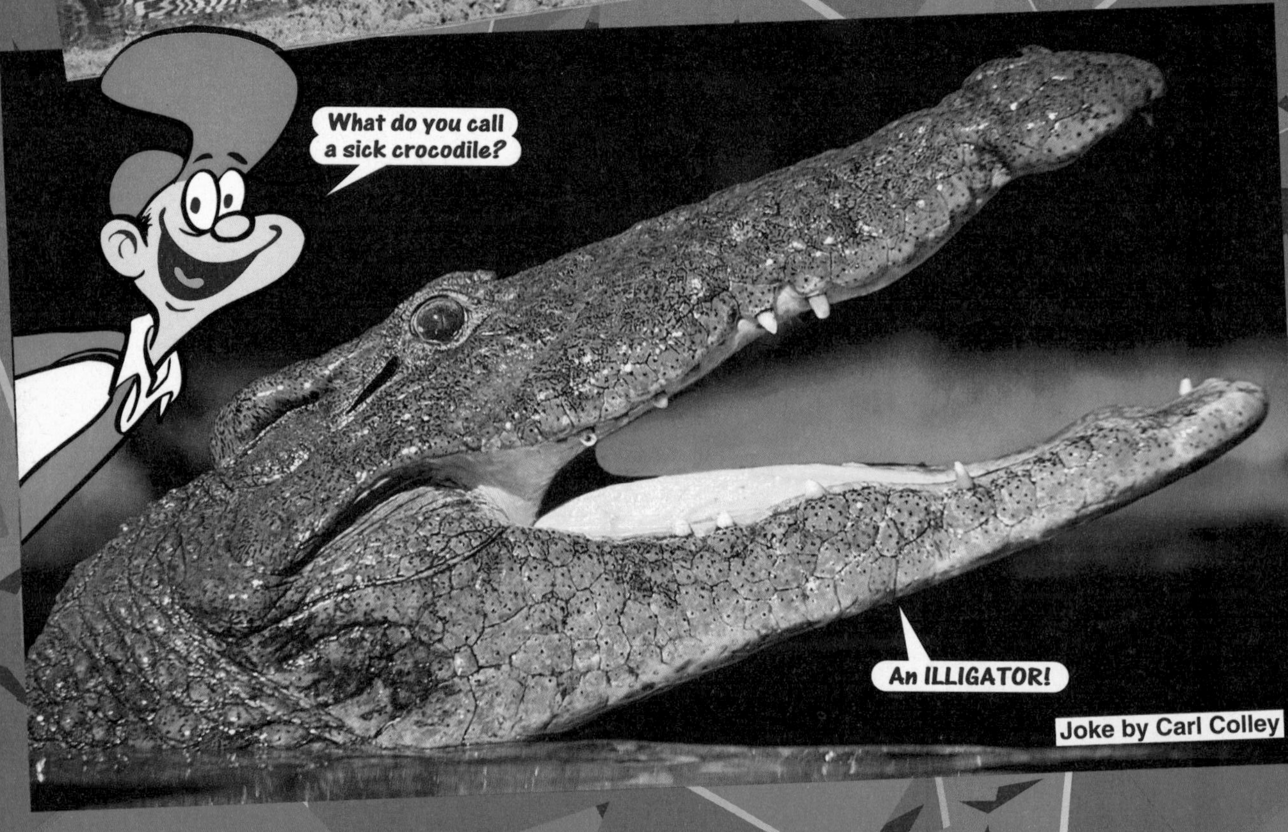

IVY the TERRIBLE in— MOOR'S THE MERRIER

WE'RE ON A CAMPING HOLIDAY! KEEP UP, IVY!

BAH! I WANTED A HOLIDAY IN A POSH HOTEL WITH BEDS AND T.V. AND STUFF!

BUT THIS IS DARTMOOR! ALL THERE IS ARE GHOSTS! CREEPY MIST! THE HOUND OF THE BASKERVILLES! GAH!

THUD! THUD!

RUBBISH! IT'S A LOVELY, SUNNY DAY. LET'S SET UP CAMP!

IF WE MUST.

MAYBE IT'S SUNNY NOW. BUT IT'LL BE A CREEPY NIGHT. AND THAT'S A PROMISE!

THIS BIT WHERE?

So, at night —

'NIGHT-'NIGHT!

SLEEP WELL, IVY!

TIME FOR A LAUGH, PALS. DEODORANTS FIRST.

IT'S GETTING MISTY, DAD!

HISS!

HISS!

CREEPY, HUH?

COUGH! COUGH!

WOW! STAY IN YOUR TENT, IVY.

I THINK I CAN HEAR THE HOUND OF THE BASKERVILLES!

HOWWWLL! SCREEECH!

TWIDDLE! PRESS

EEK! THE HOUND! IT'S OUT THERE! IT IS!

WHAT'S ALL THIS NOISE ABOUT?

NO SUCH THING! WHAT HA YOU FOUND, HENRY?

SNIFF!

THE HOUND OF THE BASKERVILLES IS AFTER US!

OI! GERROFF!

OO-ER! RUMBLED!

SO! IT WAS YOU!

PSST! CAN YOU HELP?

SURE!

'BYE!

WELL, IVY HAS GOT A NIGHT IN A BIG HOTEL!

YEAH! AND WE CAN GO CAMPING.

DARTMOOR PRISON

HEE-HEE! WE'RE GUARDS AT DARTMOOR'S BIGGEST 'HOTEL'.

HEY! LET ME OUT! THIS ISN'T MY IDEA OF A HOTEL!

NO T.V. AND BREAD AND WATER FOR YOUR BREAKFAST! NICE COMFY CELL YOU'VE GOT, THOUGH!

HE MUST BE EXPECTING A DIRTY GAME — LOOK AT THE SIZE OF THOSE SHINPADS!

BALL BOY GETS SPORTY!

THEY'RE ALL USING THEIR HANDS — FOULS ALL ROUND!

AWFUL SMALL PITCH, THIS!

SURELY THIS GAME MUST BE ABANDONED — PITCH FLOODED!

HEY! THERE ARE TOO MANY CORNER FLAGS ON THIS PITCH!

S.N.S.C. 40

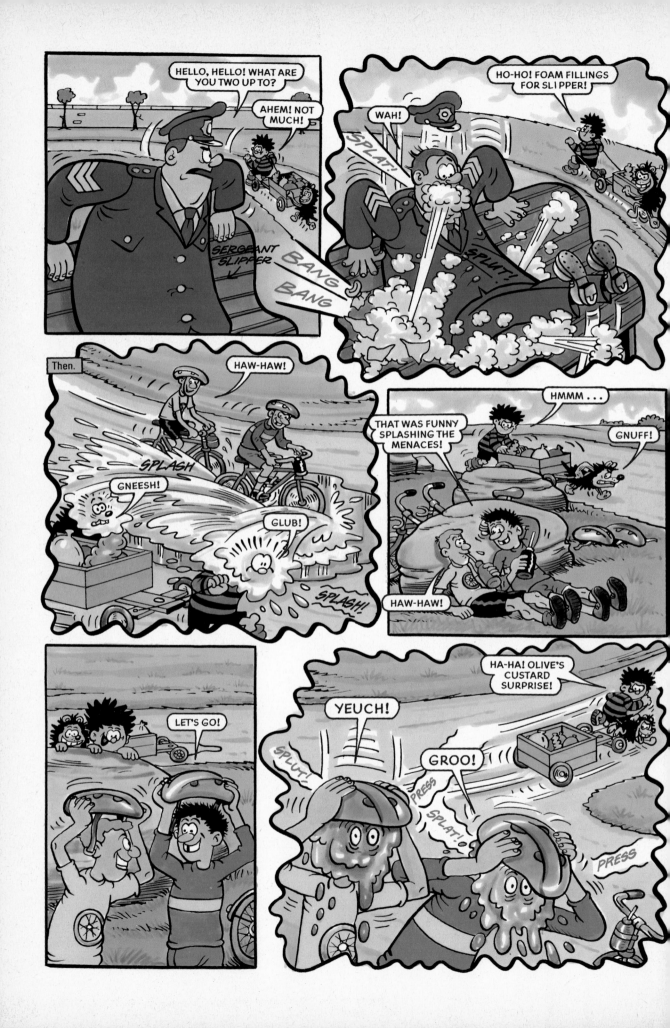

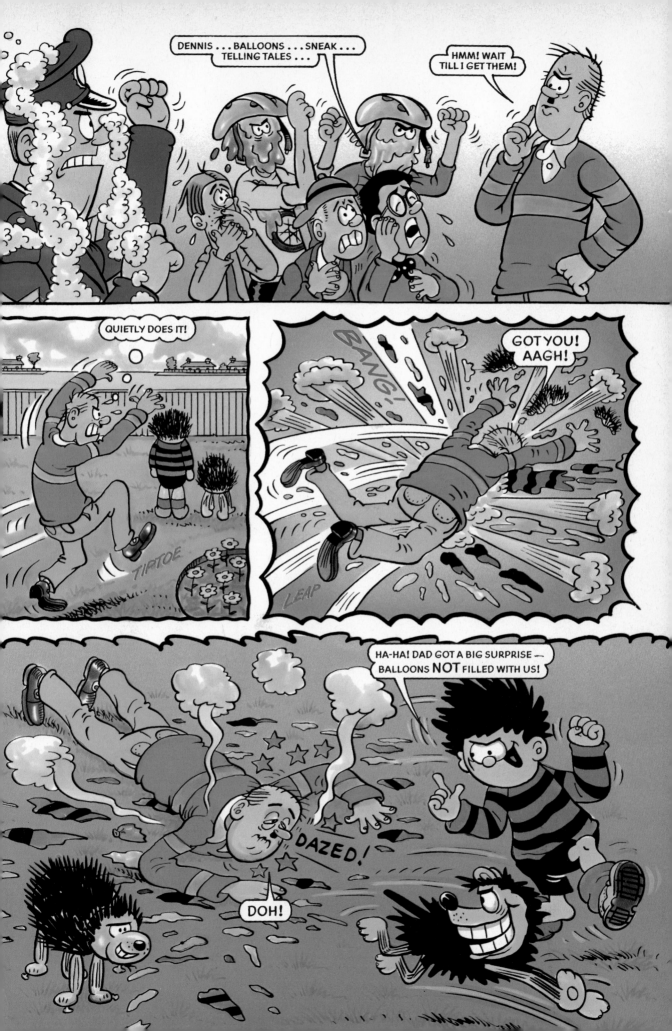